Let's Discover The States

The Great Plains

MONTANA • NEBRASKA • NORTH DAKOTA
SOUTH DAKOTA • WYOMING

By
Thomas G. Aylesworth
Virginia L. Aylesworth

CHELSEA HOUSE PUBLISHERS
New York   Philadelphia

Created and produced by Blackbirch Graphics, Inc.

DESIGN: Richard S. Glassman
PROJECT EDITOR: Bruce S. Glassman
ASSOCIATE EDITOR: Robin Langley Sommer

3 5 7 9 8 6 4 2

Printed in the United States

Library of Congress Cataloging-in-Publication Data

Aylesworth, Thomas G.
    The Great Plains.

    (Let's discover the states)
    Includes bibliographies and index.
    Summary: Discusses the geographical, historical, and cultural aspects of Montana, Nebraska, North Dakota, South Dakota and Wyoming, using maps, illustrated fact spreads, and other illustrated material to highlight the land, history, and people of each individual state.
    1. West (U.S.)—Juvenile literature. 2. Montana—Juvenile literature. 3. North Dakota—Juvenile literature. 4. South Dakota—Juvenile literature. [1. Great Plains. 2. Montana. 3. North Dakota. 4. South Dakota]
I. Aylesworth, Virginia L. II. Title. III. Series.
F597.A95 1988   978   87-18198
ISBN 1-55546-566-8
        0-7910-0535-6 (pbk.)

CONTENTS

The crystal clear water of Lake Josephine in Glacier National Park.

Patterns formed by strips of wheat on the vast farms near Great Falls.

The gleaming copper dome of the state capitol in Helena.

The surging waters of the Gallatin, the Madison, and the Jefferson Rivers as they meet to form the Missouri River near Three Forks.

The majesty of Fort Peck Dam—the world's largest earth-fill dam—stretching for miles across the prairie.

The thrills of downhill skiing in the mountains near Whitefish.

Let's Discover

Montana

MONTANA

At a Glance

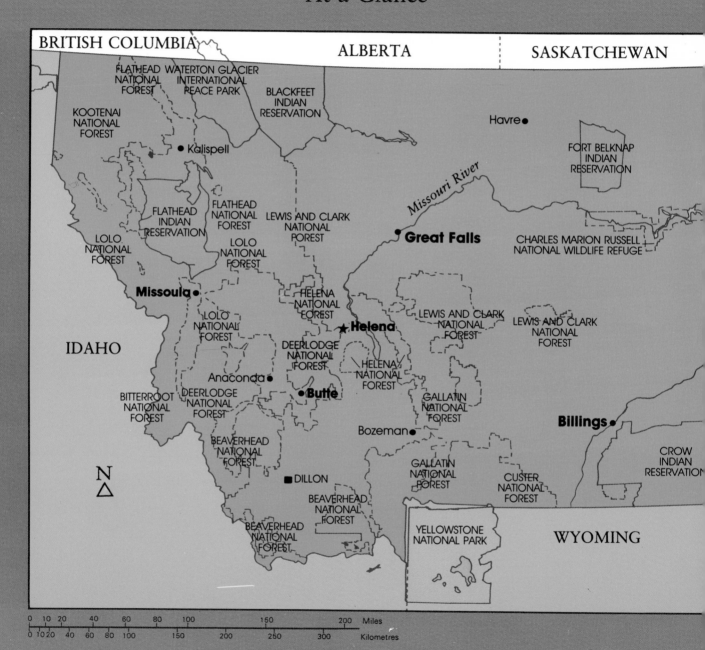

BRITISH COLUMBIA
ALBERTA
SASKATCHEWAN

FLATHEAD NATIONAL FOREST

WATERTON GLACIER INTERNATIONAL PEACE PARK

BLACKFEET INDIAN RESERVATION

KOOTENAI NATIONAL FOREST

Havre●

FORT BELKNAP INDIAN RESERVATION

●Kalispell

FLATHEAD INDIAN RESERVATION

FLATHEAD NATIONAL FOREST

LEWIS AND CLARK NATIONAL FOREST

Missouri River

LOLO NATIONAL FOREST

LOLO NATIONAL FOREST

●Great Falls

CHARLES MARION RUSSELL NATIONAL WILDLIFE REFUGE

Missoula●

LOLO NATIONAL FOREST

HELENA NATIONAL FOREST

★Helena

LEWIS AND CLARK NATIONAL FOREST

LEWIS AND CLARK NATIONAL FOREST

IDAHO

DEERLODGE NATIONAL FOREST

HELENA NATIONAL FOREST

Anaconda●

BITTERROOT NATIONAL FOREST

DEERLODGE NATIONAL FOREST

●Butte

GALLATIN NATIONAL FOREST

Billings●

Bozeman●

N
△

BEAVERHEAD NATIONAL FOREST

■DILLON

GALLATIN NATIONAL FOREST

CUSTER NATIONAL FOREST

CROW INDIAN RESERVATION

BEAVERHEAD NATIONAL FOREST

YELLOWSTONE NATIONAL PARK

WYOMING

BEAVERHEAD NATIONAL FOREST

0 10 20   40   60   80   100   150   200   Miles
0 10 20 40   60   80 100   150   200   250   300   Kilometres

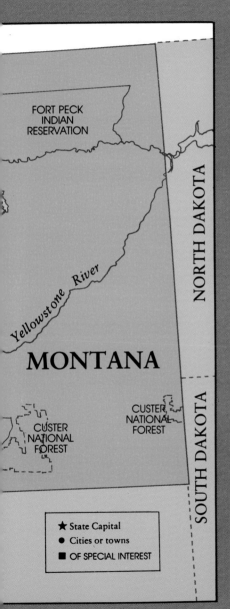

FORT PECK INDIAN RESERVATION

NORTH DAKOTA

Yellowstone River

MONTANA

CUSTER NATIONAL FOREST

CUSTER NATIONAL FOREST

SOUTH DAKOTA

★ State Capital
● Cities or towns
■ OF SPECIAL INTEREST

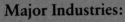

Capital: Helena

Major Industries:
Lumber, mining, metallurgy, petroleum, agriculture, livestock

Major Crops:
Grains, sugar beets, hay, flax

State Flag

Size: 147,138 square miles (4th largest)
Population: 824,000 (44th largest)

State Bird:
Western Meadowlark

The Missouri River originates in Montana at the junction of the Gallatin, Jefferson, and Madison Rivers. From here it flows north and then east to irrigate much of northern Montana. The Missouri is the country's second longest river and a major artery of trade and commerce.

The Bighorn Canyon National Recreation Area is located in the southernmost part of the state, near Montana's border with Wyoming.

The Land

Montana is bounded on the west and southwest by Idaho, on the southeast by Wyoming, on the east by North and South Dakota, and on the north by the Canadian provinces of British Columbia, Alberta, and Saskatchewan. There are two major land regions in the state: the Great Plains and the Rocky Mountains.

The Great Plains make up the eastern three-fifths of Montana. This gently rolling highland is part of the vast Interior Plain of North America, which stretches from Canada to Mexico. The land here is ideal for grain crops and for sheep and cattle ranching. There are also oil wells in the region. The terrain is varied by hills and wide river valleys, with occasional mountains.

The Rocky Mountains cover western Montana, forming a landscape of striking beauty. Grassy valleys and towering mountains, evergreen forests and sparkling lakes make up the scenery. On the highest peaks is perpetual snow, and there are a few active glaciers and many permanent snow fields. The most important of the more than 50 mountain ranges in the region are the Absaroka, Beartooth, Beaverhead, Big Belt, Bitterroot, Bridger, Cabinet, Flathead, Gallatin, Little Belt, Madison, Mission, Swan, and Tobacco Root. It is a region of forest products and asbestos, gold, zinc, manganese, silver, lead, and copper mines.

Three important river systems drain the state: the Missouri, including its Yellowstone branch; the Columbia; and the Nelson-Saskatchewan systems. Montana has only one large natural lake—Flathead Lake in the northwest, which covers about 189 square miles. But there are numerous smaller lakes, including 250 in Glacier National Park alone.

Montana's weather varies markedly from east to west. Temperatures west of the Continental Divide (the land elevation that separates waters running west to the Pacific Ocean from those running east to the Atlantic) are warmer in winter and cooler in summer than those in the east. Temperatures average 12 to 31 degrees Fahrenheit in January and 54 to 84 degrees F. in July. Snowfall is heavy in all parts of the state, with over 30 inches per year in the northwest—and 300 inches is not unheard of. An unusual climatic feature of Montana is the *chinook*—warm dry wind blowing down the eastern slopes of the mountains—which enables farmers to graze cattle on the ranges for short periods during the winter.

Below left:
The bison was once a common sight on the great plains of Montana. Today, it is almost extinct, along with the endangered kit fox, gray wolf, fisher, and Audubon sheep. Montana remains one of the nation's safest habitats for such animals as the buffalo, beaver, grizzly and black bear, moose, elk, coyote, and mountain lion.

Below:
The Pintler Scenic Route in the southwestern part of the state, meanders through high mountain passes and along the shores of Georgetown Lake.

The History

Above:
The great explorers Lewis and Clark first entered Montana in April 1805, traveling west on the Missouri River from the mouth of the Yellowstone.

Below:
A Crow Indian painting of a buffalo hunter. The Crow and other tribes such as the Cheyenne, Shoshone, Sioux, Mandan, and Nez Percé were encountered in the Montana region by 18th-century explorers.

There were two groups of Indian tribes living in what is now Montana before the white man came. On the eastern plains were the Arapaho, the Assiniboin, the Blackfoot, the Cheyenne, and the Crow. In the western mountains were the Bannock, the Kalispel, the Kutenai, and the Shoshone. Other Great Plains Indians, including the Sioux, the Mandan, and the Nez Percé, came into the region to hunt buffalo and other game.

The French traders Pierre and François de la Vérendrye visited what is now Montana in 1743, but the area was largely unexplored and unknown until most of it was acquired by the United States as part of the Louisiana Purchase from France in 1803. Meriwether Lewis and William Clark led their party of explorers through the Montana region in 1805, opening a trail to the Pacific Ocean. They discovered what would be a famous landmark for later pioneers: 200-foot Pompey's Pillar, a gigantic rock rising above the Yellowstone River.

Two years later, in 1807, the establishment of Manuel Lisa's trading post at the mouth of the Big Horn River ushered in a half century of hunting and trapping. In 1847 the American Fur Company built the first permanent settlement in Montana at Fort Benton on the Missouri River. Then, in 1862, gold was discovered in Grasshopper Creek in southwestern Montana. When other strikes followed, the region was stampeded by gold seekers, with picturesque and lawless frontier towns springing up as fast as miners could build them: Virginia City, Bannack, Diamond City, and others. Until this time, Montana had been part of the Idaho Territory, but the high crime rate in the mining camps and towns necessitated closer governing, so the Montana Territory was created by the federal government in 1864.

Above:
General George Armstrong Custer, who led the U.S. 7th Cavalry at the Battle of Little Bighorn.

At left:
A U.S. military campaign was launched against the Sioux and Cheyenne Indians in 1876 to counter the growing threat of tribes angered by the careless slaughter of buffalo by white settlers and by U.S. violations of treaties. The Battle of Little Bighorn on June 25, 1876, seen here, was one of the Indians' last but greatest victories over the white man. More than 200 men of the U.S. 7th Cavalry, led by General George Armstrong Custer, met overwhelming numbers of Sioux and Cheyenne, led by Crazy Horse and Sitting Bull, along the Little Bighorn River, and Custer's entire command was annihilated. The battle is frequently referred to as "Custer's Last Stand."

Cattle ranching became important after the first longhorn herd was brought up from Texas in 1866 by a cattleman named Nelson Story. These thousand head of cattle gave a strong impetus to the ranching industry already established in the mountain valleys, and extension of the railroads into Montana made cattle raising even more profitable. But the extremely cold winter of 1886–87 killed thousands of animals and reduced the industry considerably.

Throughout this period the Indians were being pushed farther and farther west, off land that had been their own. Two of the most notorious Indian campaigns in American history were fought in the Montana Territory. On June 25, 1876, Custer's Last Stand was made near the Little Bighorn River in southern Montana. Part of the U.S.

Chief Joseph, known to his people as Hinmaton-Yalakit, led the Nez Percé Indians in their attempted flight to Canada to avoid eviction from their Wallowa Valley homeland to Idaho reservations. At Bear Paw Mountain in Montana, after a 1,000-mile retreat marked by 13 engagements with U.S. troops, Joseph and his followers were forced to surrender in 1877 and to give up all rights to their native territories.

7th Cavalry, led by the reckless general George A. Custer, was wiped out by Sioux and Cheyenne warriors under Crazy Horse, Gall, and Two Moons. The second action was the two-day battle at Big Hole in southwestern Montana in 1877. Chief Joseph of the Oregon Nez Percé was trying to lead his tribe through the territory to safety in Canada to avoid resettlement on a reservation. The thousand-mile flight of the Nez Percé ended at Big Hole with surrender to federal troops led by Colonel Nelson A. Miles.

Montana became the 41st state in 1889, after its population had risen to some 140,000. During the 1880s and 1890s silver was discovered in the rock ledges of Butte Hill. Then rich veins of copper were unearthed nearby. Smelters were built to refine the ore, and Butte Hill became known as "the Richest Hill on Earth."

During the early 1900s, Montana began to make increasing use of its rich natural resources. Dams were built, the railroads were extended, and new plants refined sugar, milled flour, and processed meat. The magnificent Glacier National Park was created in 1910. On the political side, Jeannette Rankin of Missoula was elected to the United States House of Representatives in 1916—several years before suffrage was granted to women on a national level.

During the Great Depression of the 1930s, Montana suffered primarily from the lack of demand for its metals. But the economy boomed again during World War II, when metals, grains, and meat were needed in great quantities for the war effort. In recent years the state has become popular with vacationers because of its breathtaking natural beauty and outdoor recreational activities.

Montana's first schools were started in the mining camps of the 1860s, but they were privately owned and charged tuition. It was not until 1893 that the state guaranteed free public education. The first institution of higher education in Montana was Rocky Mountain College (1883). Ten years later, colleges and universities increased dramatically. Founded in 1893 were the University of Montana, Montana College of Mineral Science and Technology, Montana State University, and Western Montana College.

Far left:
American Indians are inseparable from Montana's cultural heritage. The Indian population, which has increased steadily since the 1950s, now constitutes the most significant ethnic minority in the state.

At left:
Screen legend Gary Cooper, born in Helena, was a cowboy before he went to Hollywood. Known for his low-key acting style, Cooper won Academy Awards for his roles in the films *Sergeant York* and *High Noon*.

The People

About 53 percent of the people of Montana live in cities and towns, of which Billings and Great Falls are the largest. The majority of them are Protestants, but the Roman Catholic community is the largest single religious group. Montana's Indian peoples now live mainly on 5 million acres of reservation land populated by the Blackfoot, Crow, Confederated Salish and Kootenai, Assiniboin, Gros Ventre, Sioux, Northern Cheyenne, Chippewa, and Cree tribes. Almost half the state's people still live in agricultural areas.

Two historical figures—both of them women—stand out in Montana history. One is Jeannette Rankin (born near Missoula), the only member of Congress to vote against United States participation in the two World Wars—a courageous stand for the times. "Calamity Jane" Cannary, the almost mythological frontier woman who traveled with "Wild Bill" Hickok's Wild West show, spent her youth in Virginia City. The state has also given us three entertainment legends—Gary Cooper (Helena), Myrna Loy (Helena), and Martha Raye (Butte).

Glacier National Park.

The Custer Battlefield
National Monument, near
Hardin.

IN NORTHWESTERN MONTANA: *Glacier National Park*
One million acres of majestic mountain scenery, including several peaks that have
never been climbed.

NEAR GREAT FALLS: *Great Falls of the Missouri*
This is the highest waterfall on the Missouri River, dropping 400 feet over eight
miles.

IN SOUTHWESTERN MONTANA: *Yellowstone National Park*
Most of this magnificent park is in Wyoming, but three of its five entrances are in
Montana.

NEAR DILLON: *Virginia City*
This old mining camp has been restored to look as it did in 1865, when it was one
of the world's richest gold camps.

IN ANACONDA: *Anaconda Reduction Works*
This is one of the world's largest copper smelters, with a smokestack almost 600
feet tall.

For more information write:
TRAVEL PROMOTION BUREAU
MONTANA DEPARTMENT OF COMMERCE
HELENA, MONTANA 59620

FURTHER READING

Carpenter, Allan. *Montana*, rev. ed. Childrens Press, 1979.
Fradin, Dennis B. *Montana in Words and Pictures*. Childrens Press, 1981.
Johnson, Dorothy M. *Montana*. Coward, 1971.
Lamb, Russell. *Montana*. Graphic Arts Center, 1980.
Lang, William L., and Myers, R. C. *Montana: Our Land and People*. Pruett, 1979.
Malone, Michael P., and Roeder, R. B. *Montana: A History of Two Centuries*.
University of Washington Press, 1976.

The imposing spire of Chimney Rock rising from the
flat plain at the North Platte River.

Fall football madness, as the scarlet-and-cream-clad
Cornhuskers take the field at Memorial Stadium in
Lincoln.

Traveling into the past at the Old Market in Omaha.

The Victorian elegance of William F. "Buffalo Bill"
Cody's mansion near North Platte.

The poignant memorial to Father Edward Flanagan at
Boys Town.

Let's Discover
Nebraska

NEBRASKA
At a Glance

Capital: Lincoln

State Flag

Major Industries: Agriculture, livestock, food processing, machinery, electronics

Major Crops: Corn, sorghum, wheat, soybeans

State Flower: Goldenrod

Size: 77,227 square miles (15th largest)

Population: 1,606,000 (36th largest)

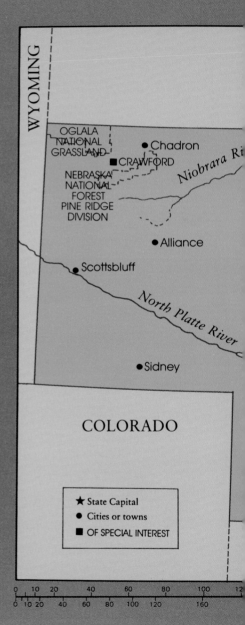

WYOMING

OGLALA NATIONAL GRASSLAND

• Chadron

■ CRAWFORD

Niobrara Ri

NEBRASKA NATIONAL FOREST PINE RIDGE DIVISION

• Alliance

• Scottsbluff

North Platte River

• Sidney

COLORADO

★ State Capital
● Cities or towns
■ OF SPECIAL INTEREST

0 10 20 40 60 80 100 12
0 10 20 40 60 80 100 120 160

SOUTH DAKOTA

IOWA

NEBRASKA NATIONAL FOREST NIOBRARA DIVISION

Elkhorn River

SANTEE INDIAN RESERVATION

South Sioux City

WINNEBAGO INDIAN RESERVATION

North Loup River

Norfolk

NEBRASKA

OMAHA INDIAN RESERVATION

NEBRASKA NATIONAL FOREST BESSEY DIVISION

Middle Loup River

Missouri River

Columbus

Fremont

Omaha

North Platte

Bellevue

Plattsmouth

Grand Island

York

★ **Lincoln**

Lexington

Kearney

Nebraska City

Platte River

Hastings

Holdrege

Beatrice

MISSOURI

McCook

Fairbury

Falls City

KANSAS

N
△

es

Above:
The waters of the entire state drain into the Missouri River, which forms the eastern border of Nebraska. With almost 11,000 miles of rivers and streams, Nebraska counts water as one of its greatest natural resources. Much of this water supply comes from rain, snow, underground springs, and a huge runoff from the Rocky Mountains of Colorado, Montana, and Wyoming.

Above right:
Nebraska's sandhills area is characterized by grassy hills, small basins, wet and dry valleys, marshes, and lakes. Its sandy soil is typical of much of the state's land.

The Land

Nebraska is bounded on the west by Wyoming and Colorado, on the north by South Dakota, on the east by Iowa and Missouri, and on the south by Kansas and Colorado. The state has two major land areas, the Dissected Till Plains and the Great Plains.

The Dissected Till Plains are a section of glacier-formed lowlands in the eastern fifth of the state. It is an area of rich, hilly farmland, with vast fields of corn, oats, hay, wheat, rye, sorghum, and soybeans. Hogs, poultry, dairy cattle, and beef cattle are also raised.

The Great Plains cover the rest of the state, a region of flowing streams, abundant well water, and excellent grasses—ideal for cattle ranching. Crops of wheat, potatoes, barley, and hay are also found here. Some oil and natural-gas wells have been sunk in the region.

The principal rivers in Nebraska are the Missouri, which forms the eastern and northeastern border of the state, and the Platte, which is formed by the junction of the North and South Platte Rivers near the city of North Platte. The state has some 2,000 lakes, none of them very large.

Quick changes in temperature are not unusual in Nebraska, and are often responsible for the violent thunderstorms, hailstorms, tornadoes, and blizzards that hit the state. Hot breezes from the Gulf of Mexico can make summer weather uncomfortable in eastern Nebraska. In July, temperatures average 78 degrees Fahrenheit, and in January, 22 degrees F., with rainfall ranging between 18 and 27 inches yearly (higher in the east).

The History

The discovery of ancient tips for stone tools and weapons indicates that there were prehistoric Indians living in what was to become Nebraska between 10,000 and 25,000 years ago. When the first white men arrived in the territory, they found several Indian tribes. Some were peaceful farmers and hunters who lived along the rivers: tribes like the Missouri, the Omaha, the Oto, and the Ponea. The Pawnee were hunters and farmers, too, but they were fierce warriors who fought with the Sioux, who lived farther north. The Pawnee became friendly with the incoming white settlers, and Pawnee scouts would help the United States Army in wars against the Sioux during the 1800s.

To the west were the Arapaho, the Cheyenne, the Comanche, and the Sioux, hunting tribes who did not farm and dwelled in temporary villages. As white settlers drove other tribes from their land on the east, several tribes migrated into the Nebraska region. Among them were the Fox, the Iowa, and the Sauk in the 1830s, and the Santee Sioux in 1863. The last to settle were the Winnebago, who were driven from Wisconsin to Iowa, then to Minnesota, then to South Dakota; they finally arrived in Nebraska in 1863 and 1864.

Francisco Vásquez de Coronado, the Spanish explorer, led an expedition into mid-America in 1541, coming up from the southwest as far as Kansas. He claimed all this territory (including present-day Nebraska) for Spain, but the Spanish government made no settlements. In 1682 the French explorer Robert Cavelier (called La Salle) traveled down the Mississippi River and claimed all the land drained by the river for France, naming this huge expanse Louisiana. French traders and fur trappers moved in during the 1690s and early 1700s, and in 1714 Étienne Veniard de Bourgmont traveled up the Missouri River to the mouth of the Platte. Spain still felt that it controlled the region, and objected to the French invasion. In 1720 a

The famous Pony Express, which ran in part through southern Nebraska, was a mail-delivery service operated by rugged young horsemen who carried packages and letters from St. Joseph, Missouri, to Sacramento, California. Each rider changed horses every 10 miles and covered a distance of some 75 miles before being relieved by another, who seized the mail pouch and dashed off to continue the journey. Armed with knives and pistols, these daring young men rode day and night through hostile Indian country and covered almost 2,000 miles in 8 to 10 days.

Spanish expedition led by Pedro de Villasur marched from Santa Fe (now in New Mexico) to Nebraska, where they were defeated by a group of Pawnee Indians and forced to retreat.

Perhaps the first white men to cross the Nebraska region were Pierre and Paul Mallet, French explorers, in 1739. France gave the Louisiana Territory to Spain in 1762, but French trappers and fur traders continued to operate in the Nebraska region, and the Spaniards never could set up a proper government in the vast wilderness. In 1800 the ruler of France, Napoleon Bonaparte, forced Spain to return Louisiana, and three years later he sold the territory to the United States.

President Thomas Jefferson sent Meriwether Lewis and William Clark on their famous expedition of 1804–06, and they explored the eastern edge of Nebraska. Another American explorer, Zebulon M. Pike, traversed the south-central part of the territory in 1806. A Spanish-American trader named Manuel Lisa set up fur-trading posts along the Missouri River between 1807 and 1820, and the Oregon Trail was opened by fur agent Robert Stuart en route from the Astoria fur-trading post in Oregon to New York City. But because of its semi-arid prairies, travelers through Nebraska considered it unfit for farming—they called it "the Great American Desert."

In 1823 the U.S. Army established Fort Atkinson on the Missouri River, about 16 miles north of present-day Omaha. The fort was the site of Nebraska's first school, library, sawmill, gristmill, and brickyard. In 1823 the first permanent settlement was established at Bellevue, near Omaha.

The Kansas-Nebraska Act of 1854 created the Kansas and Nebraska Territories, and the Nebraska Territory included not only present-day Nebraska, but also most of Montana, North Dakota, South Dakota, Wyoming, and Colorado. According to local legend, the border between the Kansas and Nebraska Territories was determined by Febold Feboldson, "the Paul Bunyan of the Great Plains," who wanted an absolutely straight border. As legend has it, he bred bees with eagles for 15 years, until he had an eagle-sized bee. He then hitched it to a plow and made a "beeline" between the two territories.

Early settlers, called "sodbusters," built sod houses and attempted to conquer the prairies. The 1862 Homestead Act, giving 160 acres of western frontier country to every settler, brought a rush of homesteaders. In 1865 the Union Pacific Railroad began laying track

Above:
William Jennings Bryan, one of the nation's greatest political orators, came to Nebraska in 1887 as a practicing lawyer. After serving as a representative to Congress (1891–95), Bryan ran unsuccessfully for a seat in the Senate. He later became editor-in-chief of the Omaha *World Herald*. In 1896 Democratic Party members who favored currency based on silver rather than gold planned to nominate Bryan for the presidency. At the party's convention that year, Bryan delivered what is commonly acknowledged as the most impressive speech ever heard at a national convention. The enthusiasm he generated was such that Bryan won the nomination, but he lost the election to William McKinley. After two more unsuccessful tries for the presidency, Bryan was appointed Secretary of State under Woodrow Wilson and was influential as an advocate for farmers and laborers and a supporter of Wilson's social-reform measures.

At right:
William Frederick Cody, better known as "Buffalo Bill," was perhaps the West's most renowned scout, hunter, and showman. He began his great "Wild West" exhibition near North Platte, Nebraska, in 1883. The show, which toured throughout the country, glorified Buffalo Bill's exploits with the Indians and his prowess as a buffalo hunter.

COL. W.F. CODY

I AM COMING

Father Edward Joseph Flanagan founded the Boys Town orphanage for underprivileged youngsters near Omaha, Nebraska. After winning national recognition for fostering leadership in his boys, he was sent by the U.S. government to Europe and the Far East after World War II to help establish orphanages for the needy abroad.

westward from Omaha, and in 1867 Nebraska became the 37th state in the Union.

After a brief setback in the 1870s, when grasshoppers ruined the crops, a second wave of settlers began to arrive. Demand for land raised prices and credit purchases became common, until drought collapsed the market in the 1890s. Irrigation, cooperatives, and conservative farming methods helped strengthen the economy after 1900, and Nebraska began to prosper. Where crops could not be grown, cattle were raised.

Nebraska was extremely hard hit by the Great Depression of the 1930s. Farm prices fell, as they did everywhere, but Nebraska was also going through another period of drought. In 1934 Nebraska approved the adoption of a unicameral state legislature—having only one house instead of the two that are used by the other 49 states.

Manufacturing, oil, and natural gas all became more important industries in Nebraska during World War II, and wartime food shortages were a boon to the state's farmers. Corn, wheat, oats, and potatoes were produced in record-breaking quantities. Today, Nebraska remains essentially an agricultural state, but its economy is shifting toward manufacturing, with emphasis on food products, machinery, metal goods, and electronics.

Nebraskans have always been vitally interested in education. After the first school was established at Fort Atkinson, mission schools for the Indians were set up by various religious groups. The first legislature of the Nebraska Territory passed a free-school law in 1855. The first institution of higher education, Doane College, was established in 1858, nine years before Nebraska became a state. Higher education blossomed, and by the turn of the century, 11 more colleges and universities had been founded: Peru State College (1867), the University of Nebraska (1869), Creighton University (1878), Duchesne College of the Sacred Heart (1881), Hastings College (1882), Dana College (1884), Midland Lutheran College (1887), Nebraska Wesleyan University (1887), Union College (1891), Wayne State College (1891), and Concordia Teachers College (1894).

The People

About 63 percent of the people in Nebraska live in cities and towns, and some 97 percent were born in the United States. Nebraska's largest communities include Omaha, Lincoln, Sioux City, Brownville, and Blair. Almost one-third of the state's population is of German descent. Protestants make up the largest religious group in the state, although there are many Roman Catholics, especially in urban areas. The largest Protestant body is the Lutheran Church; others include Baptists, Disciples of Christ, Episcopalians, Methodists, Presbyterians, and members of the United Church of Christ.

Several towering figures in American history have come from Nebraska. One important statesman represented Nebraska in Congress and ran for president as a spokesman for the free coinage of silver as well as gold: William Jennings Bryan of Lincoln, called "the Boy Orator of the Platte." The renowned legal authority Roscoe Pound was also born in Lincoln. Oglala Sioux leader Red Cloud was born along the South Platte River. Novelist Willa Cather (*My Antonia, Death Comes for the Archbishop*) lived in Nebraska and chronicled pioneer days in the West. Black civil-rights leader Malcolm X was born in Omaha.

Many actors and actresses have left Nebraska for Broadway and Hollywood. Among them are Henry Fonda (Grand Island), Marlon Brando (Omaha), Fred Astaire (Omaha), Harold Lloyd (Burchard), James Coburn (Laurel), Sandy Dennis (Hastings), and Nick Nolte (Omaha). Other show-business luminaries include television host Dick Cavett (Gibbon), puppeteer Bil Baird (Grand Island), and songwriter, singer, and actor Paul Williams (Omaha).

Above:
Stage and screen actor Henry Fonda was a native of Grand Island, Nebraska. He often portrayed men of integrity and warmth in his more than 70 films.

Below:
Malcolm X, born Malcolm Little in Omaha, Nebraska, in 1925, was a prominent black activist during the 1960s. An aggressive and articulate speaker, Malcolm X was assassinated in February 1965, while addressing a rally in New York City.

Boys Town, in Omaha.

OF SPECIAL INTEREST

NEAR OMAHA: *Boys Town*
Founded by Father Edward Flanagan in 1917 as a home for homeless and underprivileged boys, it is now a flourishing institution housing young people of many races and creeds.

NEAR NORTH PLATTE: *Scouts Rest Ranch*
The spacious Victorian-style home of William F. "Buffalo Bill" Cody, who originated his famous Wild West Show here.

IN BELLEVUE: *The Old Town*
Bellevue was the first town in Nebraska, established in 1823 as a fur-trading post. Some of its buildings are more than 100 years old.

NEAR CRAWFORD: *Toadstool Park*
Located in the Badlands of northwestern Nebraska, this park contains huge, oddly shaped rock formations carved by rain, snow, and frost.

IN LINCOLN: *State Capitol*
Rated in a poll of 500 noted architects as one of the best-built buildings in the world, Nebraska's capitol features a beautiful 400-foot central tower and fine sculpture.

For more information write:
THE DEPARTMENT OF ECONOMIC DEVELOPMENT
BOX 94666
Centennial Mall South
Lincoln, Nebraska 68509

FURTHER READING

Bailey, Bernadine. *Picture Book of Nebraska*, rev. ed. Whitman, 1966.
Carpenter, Allan. *Nebraska*, rev. ed. Childrens Press, 1979.
Creigh, Dorothy Weyer. *Nebraska: A Bicentennial History*. Norton, 1977.
Fradin, Dennis B. *Nebraska in Words and Pictures*. Childrens Press, 1980.
Nebraska: A Guide to the Cornhusker State. University of Nebraska Press, 1979.
Olson, James C. *History of Nebraska*, 2nd. ed. University of Nebraska Press, 1966.

Toadstool Park.

Towering oil wells rising from the plains near Tioga.
The heat, noise, and dust of a cattle ranch near
  Amidon.
Vast farms covering the rolling hills near Sheyenne.
An Indian chief in full regalia at a colorful ceremony
  on the Turtle Mountain reservation.
Hard-riding broncobusters at the exciting rodeo held
  every year at Dickinson.
The stark, sterile beauty of the Badlands.

Dakota

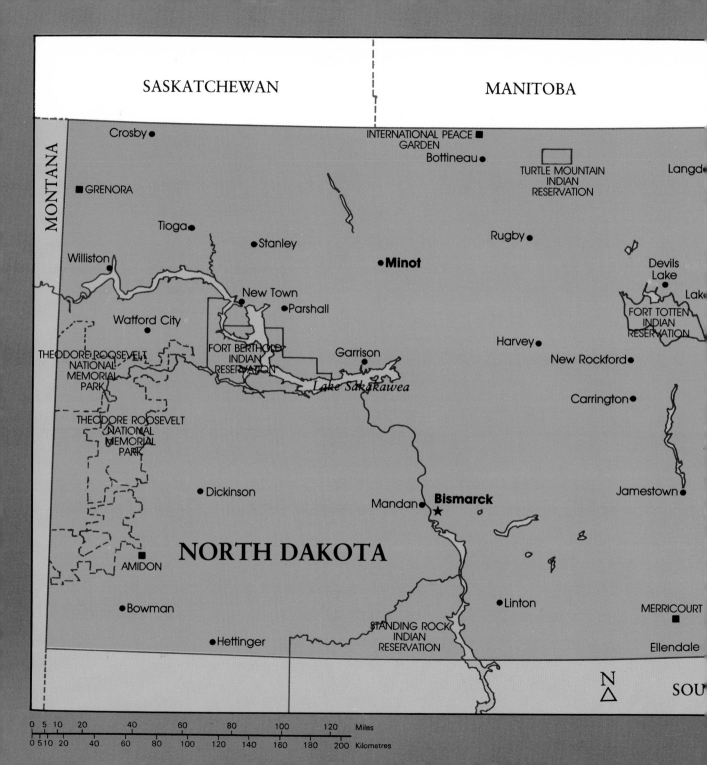

NORTH DAKOTA

At a Glance

Capital: Bismarck

Size: 70,665 square miles (17th largest)

Population: 686,000 (46th largest)

State Flag

Major Industries:
Agriculture, livestock, mining, farm equipment, processed foods

Major Crops:
Grains, potatoes, soybeans

State Flower:
Wild Prairie Rose

Map

★ State Capital
● Cities or towns
■ OF SPECIAL INTEREST

MINNESOTA

Grafton

Park River

Grand Forks
●Larimore

Mayville●

ley City
West Fargo **Fargo**

●Enderlin

●Lisbon

Wahpeton●

KOTA

At right:
By the 1980s, farms and ranches occupied more than 93 percent of North Dakota's land area and produced 10 to 15 percent of the state's total income. North Dakota is the nation's largest producer of winter wheat and durum, a hardy wheat used chiefly in making pasta. It ranks second in the United States—after Kansas—in wheat production.

Below:
Logging is only one of North Dakota's many diverse industries. Others include the mining of coal, clay, salt, and petroleum and the manufacturing of processed foods and printed material.

The Land

North Dakota is bounded on the west by Montana, on the north by the Canadian provinces of Saskatchewan and Manitoba, on the east by Minnesota, and on the south by South Dakota. The state has three major land divisions: the Red River Valley, the Young Drift Plains, and the Great Plains.

The Red River Valley is a narrow strip along the Minnesota border. It is part of an ancient glacial lake bed and has extremely fertile soil that supports dairy farms and fields of wheat, barley, rye, flax, sugar beets, soybeans, and oats. This is North Dakota's most populous area.

The Young Drift Plains are west of the Red River Valley and rise gradually toward the west and southwest. They comprise low hills of earth materials left by the glaciers (called drift) and stream-cut valleys. The Turtle Mountains are located in the northern section. This is a region of grain farms, cattle and dairy farms, and some oil wells and coal mines.

The Great Plains cover the southwestern half of the state. They are part of the huge highland that runs from Canada to southern Texas. In North Dakota they are also called the Missouri Plateau. The region's hills provide good grazing for cattle and sheep. Wheat fields are found here, as well as rich mineral deposits—uranium, natural gas, and oil.

In the southwest are the Badlands—a valley of sandstone, shale, and clay filled with weird rock formations carved by natural forces. French traders named them "bad-for-traveling."

The most important river systems in North Dakota are those of the Missouri and Red Rivers. The state has hundreds of small lakes, especially in the Young Drift Plains. One of the most unusual is Devils Lake, which has no outlet and contains water that is slightly salty.

Bitter-cold, snowy winters and warm, sunny summers are typical of the weather in North Dakota. Low humidity keeps the state cool in summer, in spite of the long hours of sunshine (North Dakota has more hours of sunlight per day than any other state). Average temperatures in July are 71 degrees Fahrenheit, and in January, 10 degrees F. Snowfall averages 37 inches per year and rain is most frequent between April and September—some 18 inches per year.

Above:
Lake Sakakawea, which covers 609 miles in the western half of North Dakota, is one of the world's largest man-made lakes. The Missouri River supplies its waters, which are contained by Garrison Dam, a huge earth-fill dam and hydroelectric-power complex.

At left:
The sun sets over North Dakota's vast, flat prairies, which typify the landscape of the state.

At right:
A Mandan warrior performing the ceremonial Dog Dance. The Mandan were primarily an agricultural people, who were farming the North Dakota region when French explorers arrived.

Far right:
A portrait of a Hidatsa chief, who led one of the many Indian tribes native to the North Dakota region. The Hidatsa, Mandan, Arikara, Sioux, Assiniboin, and Cheyenne were among the territory's first inhabitants.

The History

Most original inhabitants of what is now North Dakota were peaceful farmers living in the Missouri Valley in the south-central part of the territory. They belonged to the Arikara, Cheyenne, Hidatsa, and Mandan tribes and lived in villages that were fortified for protection from raids by the hunter and warrior tribes that occasionally came down from the northeast, such as the Assiniboin, Chippewa, and Sioux, or Dakota. After they acquired horses, which had been introduced to Central America by the Spanish *conquistadores* in the late 16th century, farming became less important. The northern Plains people became buffalo hunters like the other tribes in the region.

In 1682 the explorer Robert Cavelier (known as La Salle) claimed for France all lands along the Mississippi River and its tributaries, including the southwestern half of present-day North Dakota, whence the Missouri River flows into the Mississippi. France also laid claim to the northeastern part of the region as an extension of its Hudson Bay holdings in Canada. In 1713 France ceded the Hudson Bay territory to Great Britain.

The North Dakota area was not explored until 1738, when the French fur trader Pierre de la Vérendrye set out from Canada and reached the Mandan Indian village near present-day Bismarck. After the Louisiana Purchase of 1803, President Thomas Jefferson sent Meriwether Lewis and William Clark on their famous expedition to explore the vast territory formerly held by France. They reached central North Dakota in October 1804 and built Fort Mandan on the east bank of the Missouri River, opposite present-day Stanton. Scottish and Irish families from Canada began emigrating to North Dakota, and in 1812 they founded a settlement at Pembina. Four years later the United States obtained northeastern North Dakota from Great Britain by treaty, and by 1823 Pembina was deserted: the settlers moved back to Canada in order to remain under British rule.

It wasn't until 1861 that Congress created the Dakota Territory, which included what is now North and South Dakota and much of Montana and Wyoming. Even then, the lack of roads and railroads and fear of Indians, especially the Sioux, kept homesteaders away. During the 1860s and the 1870s, federal troops suppressed Indian uprisings against seizure of their lands and treaties broken by the government. Peace did not return until 1881, when Sioux chief Sitting Bull surrendered to U.S. soldiers.

The turning point came about 1875, when Eastern businesses and enterprising settlers established enormous wheat farms of from 3,000 to 65,000 acres, mainly in the Red River Valley. They were so successful that they were nicknamed "bonanza" farms, and stories

Sacagawea, the Shoshone woman who acted as a guide and interpreter for the explorers Lewis and Clark, joined their expedition in North Dakota in 1804. Although she set out from Fort Mandan with a month-old baby and fell sick several times, Sacagawea made the year-long journey to Oregon's Fort Clatsop and Tillamook Head. She was the only woman on the Lewis and Clark Expedition.

Fort Abercrombie, built in the southern Red River Valley in 1857, was the first military post constructed in North Dakota. Similar forts were built during this time to protect supply lines and assist pioneers, as they pushed the Indians farther west in their effort to settle the land.

about them brought thousands of settlers into the region. Because towns were growing up in distant corners of the huge Dakota Territory, where communication and transportation were difficult, settlers requested that it be divided in half. This division took place in 1889, and later that year the states of North and South Dakota were admitted to the Union. North Dakota became the 39th state.

The population of North Dakota more than doubled between 1890 and 1910, but the farmers still had to deal with Minnesota banks, grain companies, and railroads. In 1915 the Nonpartisan League was formed, which advocated state ownership of large farming facilities like grain elevators and storage plants. In 1919 the Bank of North Dakota was established, and in 1922 the North Dakota Mill and Elevator in Grand Forks began operating.

North Dakota was severely affected by the Great Depression of the 1930s, when farm production declined, residents began leaving the state, and a severe drought occurred. State and national programs to promote irrigation projects and prevent soil erosion helped farmers regain their productivity. The United States entered World War II in 1941, and North Dakota excelled in meeting the armed forces' need for farm products. In 1951 oil was discovered near Tioga, and it soon became North Dakota's most valuable mineral resource. Today, the state is moving away from its traditional dependence on agriculture and making a determined effort to foster industry. Its principal manufactured goods are farm equipment and processed foods, and vast coal fields are an important source of power.

The first school in North Dakota was established by Roman Catholic missionaries at Pembina in 1818. Public schools were mandated by the government of the Dakota Territory in 1862, and the first institution of higher education, the University of North Dakota, was founded in 1883. By the turn of the century, four more colleges and universities had been established: Jamestown College (1884), Mayville State College (1889), Valley City State College (1889), and North Dakota State University of Agriculture and Applied Science (1889).

The rugged spirit of the plains and prairies is captured by bull riding, one of the state's most popular rodeo events.

The People

Fewer than half the people in North Dakota live in cities and towns—48.8 percent. The state's population density is only 9.9 per square mile, with the largest urban areas at Fargo, Grand Forks, Minot, and Bismarck. About 95 percent of North Dakotans were born in the United States; those born in foreign countries came mainly from Canada, Germany, Norway, and Russia. More than half of the church members in the state belong to either the Roman Catholic or the Lutheran Church.

The young Shoshone woman Sacagawea, who guided the Lewis and Clark expedition, met the explorers in North Dakota. General George A. Custer and his 7th Cavalry were quartered at Fort Abraham Lincoln, in the Mandan area, during the Indian Wars of the 1870s. Prominent North Dakotans of modern times include singer Peggy Lee (Jamestown), actress Angie Dickinson (Kolm), and orchestra leader Lawrence Welk, of Strasburg. Louis L'Amour, the author of dozens of best-selling Western novels, was born in Jamestown.

A traditional Scandinavian festival. Settlers from Norway and other Scandinavian countries were among the first to farm and build on North Dakota soil. Other immigrants came from Germany and Russia.

The International Peace
Garden.

TURTLE MOUNTAINS/CANADIAN BORDER: *International Peace Garden*
This beautiful park is shared with the Canadian province of Manitoba and
symbolizes the long relationship between the United States and Canada.

NEAR GRENORA: *Writing Rock*
This large glacial boulder is covered with Indian picture writing from prehistoric
times.

IN WESTERN NORTH DAKOTA: *Theodore Roosevelt National Memorial Park*
Located in the Badlands, this is a wildlife sanctuary that contains petrified forests,
prairie dog towns, and other natural attractions.

NEAR AMIDON: *Burning Lignite Beds*
The fire in these soft-coal beds has been burning slowly but continuously for over
80 years; it can be seen for miles at night.

NEAR MERRICOURT: *Whitestone Hill*
The site of a battle in 1863 in which the Sioux were defeated by U.S. cavalrymen.

For more information write:
NORTH DAKOTA TOURISM PROMOTION
CAPITOL GROUNDS
BISMARCK, NORTH DAKOTA 58505

FURTHER READING

Bailey, Bernadine. *Picture Book of North Dakota.* Whitman, 1971.
Carpenter, Allan. *North Dakota*, rev. ed. Children Press, 1979.
Fradin, Dennis B. *North Dakota in Words and Pictures.* Childrens Press, 1981.
Robinson, Elwyn B. *History of North Dakota.* University of Nebraska Press,
1966.
Tweton, D. Jerome, and Jelliff, Theodore. *North Dakota: The Heritage of a
People.* North Dakota Institute for Regional Studies, North Dakota State
University, 1976.
Wilkins, Robert P., and Huchette, Wynona. *North Dakota: A Bicentennial
History.* Norton, 1977.

The stately memorial to four presidents carved into the
   face of Mount Rushmore near Rapid City.
Wide blue skies over a herd of cattle on the plains.
Brilliant lights illuminating the multi-domed Corn
   Palace at Mitchell.
Gaudily dressed Sioux festival dancers in Fort Sisseton
   State Park.
The forbidding "moonscape" of Badlands National
   Monument.
Bison and burros at Custer State Park.

Let's Discover

South

Dakota

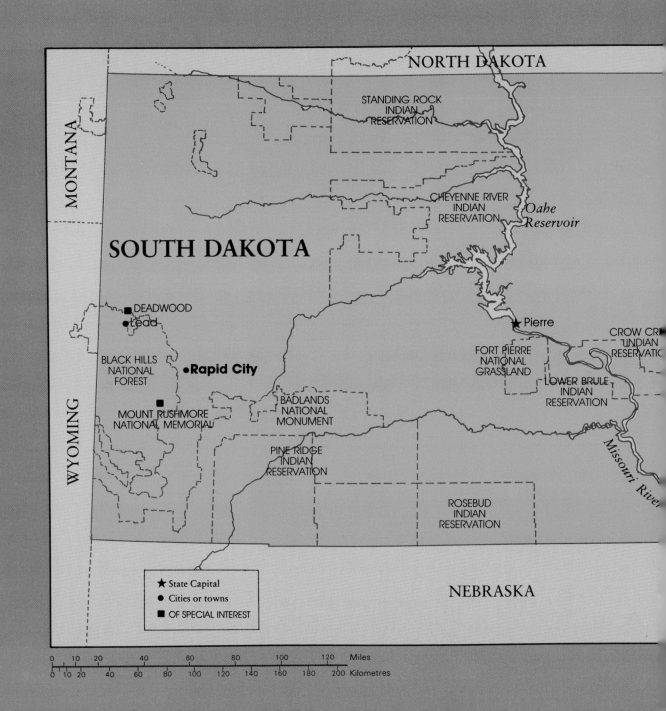

NORTH DAKOTA

STANDING ROCK
INDIAN
RESERVATION

CHEYENNE RIVER
INDIAN
RESERVATION

*Oahe
Reservoir*

SOUTH DAKOTA

■ DEADWOOD
● Lead

● **Rapid City**

BLACK HILLS
NATIONAL
FOREST

■
MOUNT RUSHMORE
NATIONAL MEMORIAL

BADLANDS
NATIONAL
MONUMENT

PINE RIDGE
INDIAN
RESERVATION

ROSEBUD
INDIAN
RESERVATION

★ Pierre

FORT PIERRE
NATIONAL
GRASSLAND

CROW CR
INDIAN
RESERVATIC

LOWER BRULE
INDIAN
RESERVATION

Missouri River

MONTANA

WYOMING

NEBRASKA

★ State Capital
● Cities or towns
■ OF SPECIAL INTEREST

| 0 | 10 | 20 | 40 | 60 | 80 | 100 | 120 | Miles |
| 0 | 10 20 | 40 | 60 | 80 | 100 120 | 140 | 160 180 | 200 Kilometres |

SOUTH DAKOTA

At a Glance

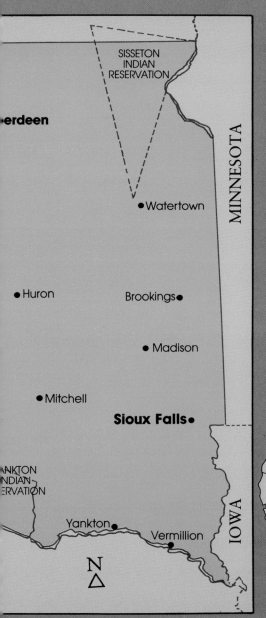

State Flower:
American Pasqueflower

State Bird:
Ring-necked Pheasant

Capital: Pierre

Major Industries: Agriculture, clothing, machinery, glass products, livestock

Major Crops: Wheat, corn, oats, hay, rye

Size: 77,047 square miles (16th largest)

Population: 706,000 (45th largest)

State Flag

The Land

South Dakota's Badlands are in the southwestern part of the state. Named for their tough terrain and difficulty of passage, the Badlands have intricate, multicolored rock formations carved by wind and water erosion. They are surrounded by a series of plateaus and studded with tall buttes and pyramids.

Corn, wheat, oats, and sunflowers are South Dakota's most important and valuable crops.

South Dakota is bounded on the west by Montana and Wyoming, on the north by North Dakota, on the east by Minnesota and Iowa, and on the south by Nebraska. There are four major land divisions in the state: the Young Drift Plains, the Dissected Till Plains, the Great Plains, and the Black Hills.

The Young Drift Plains stretch over most of eastern South Dakota, consisting of rolling hills and glacially formed lakes. This is cattle country, although many acres are given over to wheat farming.

The Dissected Till Plains form a loop in the southeastern corner of South Dakota. After the last glacier receded, streams began to cut up (dissect) till—soil, rocks, and other materials—deposited by the glaciers. The land here is good for raising beef and dairy cattle, poultry, and sheep, as well as corn, rye, hay, and oats.

The Great Plains cover most of the western two-thirds of the state and include the Badlands—rough regions made up of steep hills and deep gullies worn by wind and water. The Badlands have little economic use, but most of the Great Plains region supports cattle, sheep, and wheat. Uranium, coal, and feldspar are also mined here.

The Black Hills region consists of a low, isolated mountain group in west-central South Dakota. It is a land of great scenic beauty, with deep canyons; towering, rugged rock formations; and pine and spruce forests. There are rich mineral deposits, including gold, clay, gravel, and sand. The highest point east of the Rockies, 7,242-foot Harney Peak, is located in the Black Hills.

The most important river in South Dakota is the Missouri. Most of the state's lakes were dug by glaciers during the Ice Age. One of the most interesting is Medicine Lake, near Florence, which has a salt concentration of about four percent—higher than that of sea water.

Extremes in temperature are not uncommon in South Dakota, but even in the hottest weather, low humidity keeps the air comfortable. Temperatures often go to 100 degrees Fahrenheit in the summer and drop below 0 degrees F. in winter. The averages, however, are 74 degrees F. in July and 15 degrees F. in January. Rainfall is higher east of the Missouri, and snowfall is heaviest during February and March.

Above:
Rapid City, on the eastern edge of the Black Hills, is the second largest city in South Dakota. It has a population of over 46,000.

At left:
The combination of rolling prairies, steep rock formations, and jagged cliffs creates a dramatic landscape in South Dakota. The state flower, the pasqueflower, flourishes in its rugged surroundings.

The History

Before the white man came to what is now South Dakota, there were three major Indian tribes living in the region. The Arikara were farmers who lived near the mouth of the Cheyenne River and north of it along the Missouri. In the western part of the Cheyenne River area were the Cheyenne, farmers and hunters, who were also active along the White River and in the Black Hills. The Sioux, or Dakota, were nomadic hunters and warriors who followed the buffalo herds.

When Robert Cavelier (known as La Salle) claimed all the lands drained by the Mississippi River system in 1682, France owned what would become South Dakota. Probably the first white men to explore the territory were the French-Canadians François and Louis-Joseph de la Vérendrye, the sons of explorer Pierre de la Vérendrye. In 1743 these brothers buried an inscribed lead plate near present-day Fort Pierre to prove they had been there. This plate was not found until 1913, when schoolchildren discovered it.

In 1762 France ceded its land west of the Mississippi River to Spain, which returned it in 1800. Three years later the United States bought this vast Louisiana Territory from France, and President Thomas Jefferson sent Meriwether Lewis and William Clark on their famous exploratory trip to the Pacific Ocean. In August of 1804, Lewis and Clark camped in the South Dakota region, near what is now Elk Point, and then went on to follow the Missouri River through the territory.

After the Lewis and Clark expedition, many fur trappers entered the region, and the first permanent settlement, a trading post, was built on the site of present-day Fort Pierre in 1817. It was established by Joseph la Framboise, a French trader. Despite troubles with the Indians, which began in 1823 and lasted into the 1830s, the fur trade thrived until the 1850s, when it suffered from both dwindling supply and declining demand. During the years from 1812 to 1834, the area was part of the Missouri Territory.

An old gold mine still stands as a reminder of the great South Dakota gold rush of 1874, when gold was discovered in the Black Hills by General George Armstrong Custer and his men. In the fall of 1875, after the military ceased to uphold the treaty prohibiting white settlement in the Black Hills territory sacred to the Sioux, gold seekers poured into the area and quickly uprooted the Sioux, who surrendered their claims in 1876 after a series of uprisings.

At left:
Explorers Lewis and Clark greet Indians met on their way across the Great Plains. After President Thomas Jefferson concluded the Louisiana Purchase in 1803, he dispatched the Lewis and Clark Expedition to explore the territory. As the explorers made their journey to the Pacific, they passed through what is now South Dakota.

Below:
Calamity Jane, born Martha Jane Cannary, is perhaps America's most famous frontierswoman. At the height of South Dakota's "gold fever" in 1876, Jane arrived at Camp Deadwood, the most notorious of the lawless mining camps that dotted the Black Hills. There, she gambled at the poker tables, reputedly became Wild Bill Hickok's sweetheart, and performed in the Wild West shows.

It was during the 1850s that the development of South Dakota's agriculture began. Land promoters bought up land in 1857, establishing the towns of Sioux Falls, Medary, Yankton, Bon Homme, and Vermillion within a few years. In 1861 Congress created the Dakota Territory. But severe difficulties with the Indians, especially the Sioux, followed. The Sioux were forced to sign a treaty with the government giving land in southeastern South Dakota to the United States and restricting the tribe to reservations. Controversies over new roads and trespassing onto these Indian reservations soon led to uprisings. When gold was discovered on the Sioux reservation in the Black Hills in 1874, thousands of settlers poured in. Many who came during the gold rush stayed on to farm, and the Sioux were finally forced to relinquish their land in 1877. In 1878 came "the great Dakota boom"—a land rush in which numerous farmers

and speculators entered the state. The population swelled from 12,000 in 1870 to 348,600 in 1890, when the Indian Wars effectively ended with the massacre of Indian families at Wounded Knee. By 1886 railroads had been built across South Dakota, and many towns blossomed along the right of way.

In 1889 Congress set the present boundary between North and South Dakota, the former Dakota Territory, and in November of that year South Dakota entered the Union as the 40th state. In the early 1900s, farm land was in demand and crop prices were high. As a result, thousands of settlers came to live in the state.

Then came the Great Depression of the 1930s. Not only were South Dakota farmers faced with decreased demand and prices for their products, they were also suffering through a terrible drought coupled with a grasshopper plague that began in 1930 and lasted for 10 years.

The demand for agricultural products during World War II strengthened South Dakota's economy, and dams built by the Missouri River Basin Project created more jobs and power for the development of industry. The state has become increasingly aware of the fact that it cannot rely solely on farming, and has diversified with the manufacture of clothing, machinery, metals, and other products.

The first schoolhouse in the South Dakota region opened in 1860 in Bon Homme, but it had to be torn down within three months so that its logs could be used to build a stockade for protection against the Indians. The territorial legislature authorized a public-school system in 1862, after the first institute of higher education, Augustana College, was founded in 1860. Ten more colleges and universities opened before the turn of the century: General Beadle State College (1881), South Dakota State University (1881), Southern State College (1881), Yankton College (1881), the University of South Dakota (1882), Black Hills State College (1883), Huron College (1883), Sioux Falls College (1883), Dakota Wesleyan University (1885), and South Dakota School of Mines and Technology (1885).

U.S. cavalrymen bury Indians massacred in the 1890 Battle of Wounded Knee, in which some 200 Sioux warriors, women, and children were shot down at Wounded Knee Creek. This slaughter effectively ended Indian resistance and was the last major engagement between U.S. Army soldiers and Indians in American history.

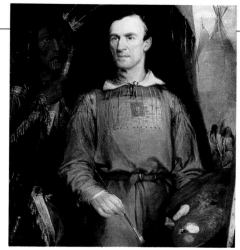

The People

Less than 50 percent of the people of South Dakota live in cities and towns, including Sioux Falls, Pierre, Rapid City, Yankton, and Vermillion. About 97 percent of South Dakotans were born in the United States. Most of those born in other countries came from Denmark, Germany, Norway, Russia, and Sweden. The largest single religious group is the Lutheran. The second largest is the Roman Catholic Church, followed by the Methodists, Presbyterians, and members of the United Church of Christ.

South Dakotans are part of our tradition of the Golden West. Hunkpapa Sioux chief Sitting Bull was born in the territory, and Oglala Sioux chief Crazy Horse lived there for years. The legendary black cowboy Deadwood Dick (Richard W. Clark) was born in Deadwood, once occupied by 7,000 lawless gold miners.

One of America's foremost scientists, Ernest O. Lawrence, the inventor of the cyclotron, was born in Canton. Novelist Laura Ingalls Wilder, born in Wisconsin, lived in De Smet and captured the pioneer spirit in her *Little House on the Prairie* and other stories for children. Actress Cheryl Ladd is a native of Huron.

Far left:
Sitting Bull, one of the most renowned Indian leaders of all time, was born near Grand River in the 1830s. As chief of the northern Sioux, he won fame as a tribal warrior in the 1860s, together with Oglala Sioux leader Crazy Horse. During the 1870s they led the confederation of Sioux, Arapaho, and Cheyenne that overwhelmed General Custer and his men at the Battle of Little Bighorn.

Above right:
George Catlin, one of America's most famous painters of the Western Indians, spent much of his career in South Dakota and other areas on the Great Plains. He was captivated by life on the prairies and dedicated himself to learning the way of life of his Indian subjects.

Below:
Traditional Czech costumes are worn at one of South Dakota's ethnic festivals. The land boom of the late 1800s brought settlers from many European countries.

Work on a gigantic carving of Oglala Sioux leader Crazy Horse has already begun at the Crazy Horse Monument site, near Custer. Seen here is the 16-foot-high model completed by sculptor Korczak Ziolkowski for the enormous sculpture in the rock of the Black Hills.

IN MITCHELL: *The Corn Palace*
This ornate building is redecorated every year with murals made of different-colored corn and other grains that have been vital to South Dakota's prosperity.

IN DEADWOOD: *Mount Moriah Cemetery*
This is the famous "Boot Hill" of Deadwood, where Wild Bill Hickok, Calamity Jane, Preacher Smith, Seth Bullock, and other colorful Western characters are buried.

NEAR RAPID CITY: *Mount Rushmore National Memorial*
The heads of four great American presidents—Washington, Jefferson, Lincoln, and Theodore Roosevelt—were carved on the face of this 6,000-foot mountain by sculptor Gutzon Borglum.

NEAR RAPID CITY: *Badlands National Monument*
A fantastic painted wasteland of steeply eroded buttes, spires, and razor-edged ridges.

WYOMING BORDER AREA: *The Black Hills*
The Needles Highway traverses this land of beautiful rock formations and towering pines.

For more information write:
TRAVEL DIRECTOR
SOUTH DAKOTA TOURISM DEVELOPMENT
PIERRE, SOUTH DAKOTA 57501

FURTHER READING

Carpenter, Allan. *South Dakota*, rev. ed. Childrens Press, 1978.

Fradin, Dennis B. *South Dakota in Words and Pictures*. Childrens Press, 1981.

Karolevitz, Robert F. *Challenge: The South Dakota Story*, 2nd ed. Brevet Press, 1979.

Milton, John R. *South Dakota: A Bicentennial History*. Norton, 1977.

Schell, Herbert S. *History of South Dakota*, 3rd ed. University of Nebraska Press, 1975.

Veglahn, Nancy. *South Dakota*. Coward, 1970.

The Teton Mountains soaring above beautiful Jackson
   Hole Valley.
The thrills of the rodeo at the Frontier Days
   celebration in Cheyenne.
Brightly costumed dancers at the All-American Indian
   Days festival at Sheridan.
The spectacular eruption of Old Faithful, Yellowstone
   National Park's most famous geyser.
Great herds of elk grazing peacefully in the meadows
   and foothills of the National Elk Refuge near
   Jackson.

Wyoming

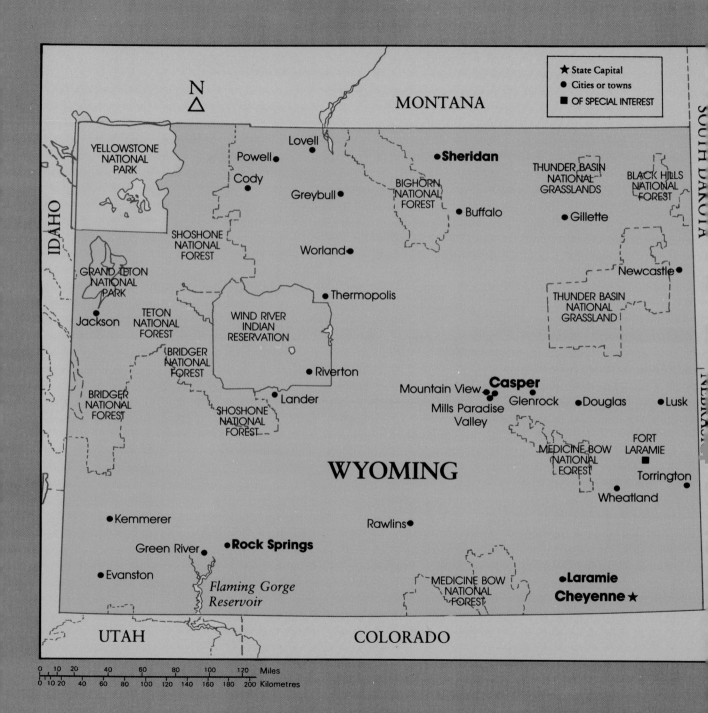

WYOMING

At a Glance

Capital: Cheyenne

State Flag

State Bird: Meadowlark

Major Industries:

Minerals, tourism, agriculture, livestock

Major Crops: Wheat, beans, barley, oats

State Motto: Equal Rights

State Tree: Cottonwood

Nicknames: Cowboy State, Equality State

State Song: "Wyoming"

Size: 97,914 square miles (9th largest)

Population: 511,000 (49th largest)

The Land

Wyoming is bordered on the west by Idaho and Utah, on the north by Montana, on the east by South Dakota and Nebraska, and on the south by Utah and Colorado. The state has three major land areas: the Great Plains, the Rocky Mountains, and the Intermontane Basins.

The Great Plains are located in a narrow strip along the eastern border, and are part of the huge interior plain of North America that extends from Canada to Mexico. Much of it is covered by short, tough grass that supports numerous cattle, sheep, and other livestock. The Black Hills are located in the northeastern part of this region and extend into South Dakota.

The Rocky Mountains sweep across the state in huge ranges. They include the Bighorn Mountains, the Laramie Range, the Granite Mountains, the Teton Ranges, and others. In the Wind River Range is the highest point in the state—13,785-foot Gannett Peak. There is some ranching and farming in the region, as well as coal mines and natural-gas and oil fields.

The Intermontane Basins consist of flat areas between the mountain ranges. Although rainfall is sparse here, the grasslands are ideal for raising cattle and sheep and irrigation has increased the land's productivity.

Parts of three great river systems begin in the mountains of Wyoming: the Missouri, the Colorado, and the Columbia systems. Many of their rivers have cut deep canyons, where spectacular waterfalls descend from high cliffs. Wyoming has hundreds of clear, cold mountain lakes.

Temperatures and weather conditions vary greatly with altitude, although generally Wyoming's climate is dry and sunny. In January, readings of 22 degrees Fahrenheit in central Wyoming and 12 degrees F. in northwestern Yellowstone National Park are not uncommon. July readings in these areas average 71 degrees F. and 59 degrees F., respectively. Snowfall is extremely high in the mountains.

Wyoming's terrain is both varied and dramatic, as a result of ancient volcanic action and erosion from rivers, streams, and mountain runoff. Floods and great surges of water through narrow channels have created deep gorges and canyons that are a breathtaking feature of the state's topography.

Wyoming contains much flatland suitable for cattle and sheep grazing.

The History

There were probably Indian hunters in what was to become Wyoming more than 11,000 years ago, and when huge herds of buffalo began roaming the prairies, they lured many tribes into the area. When the first white men arrived in the region, they found the Arapaho, Bannock, Blackfoot, Cheyenne, Crow, Flathead, Nez Percé, Shoshone, Sioux, and Ute tribes.

The first Europeans to come into the Wyoming territory may have been the French-Canadian brothers François and Louis-Joseph de la Vérendrye, who arrived in 1743. But exploration of the area did not begin until after the United States bought the Louisiana Territory, which included Wyoming, from France in 1803. After that, American trappers came in search of furs and one of them, John Colter, explored the Yellowstone region in 1807.

In 1834 Fort Laramie, the area's first permanent trading post, was established. Others, such as Fort Bridger, sprang up as the demand for furs increased, and settlers moved in to work the land. During the 1820s and 1830s, the fur trade was the most important activity in the region.

By the 1850s, a steady stream of families in covered wagons was heading westward. But the Plains Indians, alarmed at this invasion of their land, began attacking wagon trains, leading to prolonged warfare between the Indians and the United States government.

Both skirmishes and pitched battles continued until 1868, when the Sioux were forced to sign a treaty at Fort Laramie by which they gave up most of their lands except for the northeastern part of the Wyoming Territory, which was created that same year. The Indians also agreed not to interfere with track-laying for the Union Pacific Railroad through southern Wyoming. Then gold was discovered in the Black Hills in 1874, and thousands of prospectors violated the treaty by moving into the Sioux reservation. The battles between the Sioux and the U.S. cavalry began again.

A pair of knee-high moccasins crafted by Shoshone Indians of Wyoming. The Shoshone were among the many Plains Indian tribes to settle in the region, which was prized for its large herds of buffalo and other game animals.

James Bridger, a trapper and guide, was one of the most colorful figures in early Wyoming history. In 1843 he completed Fort Bridger, a trading post along the Oregon Trail. The fort later became a U.S. military post.

Several towns had been established before 1870, both along the Union Pacific tracks and along the pioneer trails that crossed the state, notably the Oregon and the Mormon Trails. The cattle industry was well established. In 1869 the territorial legislature became the first to grant women the right to vote, hold office, and serve on juries.

Wyoming became the 44th state of the Union in 1890, which opened the door to a new influx of settlers. At this point, fresh troubles arose among owners of large cattle ranches who accused newcomers of stealing from their herds. Cattle rustling led to bloodshed, including the Johnson County Cattle War of 1892.

More settlers arrived as word spread about Wyoming's excellent grazing land. Homestead acts in 1909, 1912, and 1916 provided free land for development, and the discovery of oil at Salt Creek Field near Casper in 1912 gave the economy an additional boost. Irrigation of prairie lands increased the state's agricultural output. In 1924 Wyoming elected the nation's first woman governor, Nellie Tayloe Ross. Governor Ross was elected to succeed her husband, William B. Ross, after his death earlier that year.

Wyoming was not as hard hit by the Great Depression of the 1930s as other Western states. The economy was bolstered by oil production, and the federal government constructed dams and hydroelectric stations, including those of the Kendrick Project on the North Platte River. With the coming of World War II, the state began to boom: the nation needed its coal, lumber, meat, and oil. Shortly after the war, the discovery of uranium triggered new industrial development.

Today, Wyoming remains economically sound, with tourism as a major component of its prosperity. Millions of visitors come to Yellowstone, the nation's first national park, and enjoy the other natural wonders of the state.

The first school in Wyoming was founded at Fort Laramie in 1852. The only accredited four-year university in the state is the University of Wyoming, which was established in 1887.

"Buffalo Bill" Cody, Wild West showman and scout, founded what is now the town of Cody, Wyoming, around 1895. The town was originally a large ranch established with the aid of a land grant from the state.

Wild-West rodeos are still among the most popular entertainment events in Wyoming.

The People

Almost 63 percent of the people of Wyoming live in cities and towns, and about 97 percent of them were born in the United States. Cheyenne, Laramie, and Casper are among the most populous urban areas. The largest religious groups in the state are the Baptists, Congregationalists, Episcopalians, Lutherans, Methodists, Mormons, Presbyterians, and Roman Catholics.

Famous Wyomingites include Nellie Tayloe Ross, who moved to her adopted state from St. Joseph, Missouri. Jackson Pollock, the American artist in the forefront of the abstract expressionist movement in the 1950s and 1960s, was born in Cody, the town founded by William "Buffalo Bill" Cody. Celebrated sportscaster Curt Gowdy was a native of Green River.

Yellowstone National Park has more geysers than any other site in the world.

OF SPECIAL INTEREST

NEAR FORT LARAMIE: *Fort Laramie National Historic Site*
This former fur-trading center and military post contains some of the original
    frontier buildings, which have been restored.

IN NORTHWESTERN WYOMING: *Grand Teton National Park*
The beautiful valley of Jackson Hole and the majestic Teton Mountains attract
    hikers and campers. Numerous wild animals are protected here.

IN NORTHWESTERN WYOMING: *Yellowstone National Park*
The nation's oldest and largest national park contains spectacular waterfalls and
    geysers, hot springs and canyons, and abundant wildlife.

NEAR KEMMERER: *Fossil Fish Cliff*
This cliff has fossil remains of fish that lived more than 50,000,000 years ago,
    when Wyoming was an inland sea.

IN CODY: *Buffalo Bill Historical Center*
This complex contains three museums of Western Americana—the Buffalo Bill,
    Winchester, and Plains Indian—and the Whitney Gallery of Western Art.

For more information write:
WYOMING TRAVEL COMMISSION
I–25 AT COLLEGE DRIVE
CHEYENNE, WYOMING 82002

FURTHER READING

Bailey, Bernadine. *Picture Book of Wyoming*, rev. ed. Whitman, 1972.
Bragg, William F. *Wyoming: Rugged But Right*. Pruett, 1980
Carpenter, Allan. *Wyoming*, rev. ed. Childrens Press, 1979.
Fradin, Dennis B. *Wyoming in Words and Pictures*. Childrens Press, 1980.
Lamb, Russell. *Wyoming*. Graphic Arts Center, 1978.
Larson, Taft A. *Wyoming: A Bicentennial History*. Norton, 1977.

INDEX

Numbers in italics refer to illustrations

Photo Credits/Acknowledgments

Photos on pages 5, 6–7, 9, 10, 11, 12 (top), 15 (top left), 16 courtesy of Montana Office of Tourism; pages 17, 18–19, 20, 22, 24, 25 (bottom), 26, 27 (top), 28 courtesy of Nebraska State Office of Tourism; pages 29, 30–31, 33, 34, 35, 36, 37, 38, 39, 40 courtesy of North Dakota Office of Travel and Tourism; pages 41, 42–43, 44–45, 46, 47, 48, 49 (bottom), 51 (bottom), 52 courtesy of South Dakota Office of Tourism; pages 53, 54–55, 57, 58, 61 (bottom), 62 courtesy Wyoming Office of Tourism; page 12 (bottom) New York Public Library/Stokes Collection; page 59 Museum of the American Indian; pages 13 (left), 23, 49 (top), 50, 60 Library of Congress; pages 13 (right), 14, 15 (right), 25 (top), 27 (bottom), 51 (tops), 61 (top) National Portrait Gallery, Smithsonian Institution.

Cover photograph courtesy of South Dakota Office of Tourism.

The Publisher would like to thank Sherryl Pouliot of the Montana Office of Tourism, Barbara Steinfeld of the Nebraska Office of Tourism, The North Dakota Office of Tourism, Jan Clark of the South Dakota Office of Tourism, Cindy Hendrickson of the Wyoming Office of Tourism, and Todd De-Garmo for their gracious assistance in the preparation of this book.

978   16751
Aylesworth
The Great Plains

2/91 $10.22